THE

YADA YADA

HAGGADAH

A SITCOM SEDER

Dave Cowen

CONTENTS

DISCLAIMER

This book is written as a parody of the Seinfeld television show and as a teaching tool for Judaism.

It is not authorized or endorsed by the creators, writers, producers, actors, or any of the companies or corporations involved in its production and distribution.

A portion of the profits will be donated to Jewish organizations in their honor. Don't worry, it's not The Human Fund.

Also, this Haggadah is read from left to right, because yada, yada, yada.

CAST LIST

Jerry

Larry

Stage Directions

George

Elaine

Kramer

Yael

Estelle

Frank

Ramses

Uncle Leo

Helen

Morty

Lloyd Braun

Newman

Dave Cowen

INTRODUCTION

JERRY

Hello, I'm Jerry Seinfeld[1], and I'm with my friend and collaborator, Larry David[2], to introduce our Yada Yada Haggadah. You may be wondering, how did this book come about? Well, it started when we wrote an episode of our show about our favorite Jewish holiday, Passover, called: "The Seder."

LARRY

However, the network thought it was too Jewish. So they refused to let it go on the air. Let our episode go on the air, we said. Let it go on the air, we cried out. But the network. It refused to let this episode go on the air.

JERRY

Surprisingly, G-d didn't intervene either.

---

[1]Parody, not really Jerry Seinfeld
[2] Parody, not really Larry David

LARRY

The network still doesn't want us to publish the
script. And they technically own the copyright to
our show.

JERRY

So for all these years we thought no one would
experience it. But then we read up on copyright law.
And we learned this work is protected by fair use.

LARRY

Because this is a parody that transforms the
copyrighted material into a teaching tool for
Judaism, and won't have a negative effect on the
potential market of our show, it's kosher.

JERRY

That is, unless, every Jew in the world buys a copy.

LARRY

Would that really have a negative effect on the
potential market of our 1 billion dollar show?

JERRY

Maybe. Fair use law is pretty moronic. Something's
fair use, totally fair, all fair, all well and good, until,
oops, you use it too well, it's too good, too
successful, now it's unfair. It'd be as if you had a
friend who says, go ahead, feel free to date my
ex-wife, why not, have fun. But then, when the
relationship starts going too well, you fall in love,
you ask her to marry you. A judge can rule that you
never get to see her again.

LARRY

And that you have to be your friend's butler.

JERRY

Let's get to the book already.

LARRY

Let's do it. Think of it as one big episode.
Divide up the roles from the cast list among your
Seder guests.

JERRY

Don't forget to have some people reading the stage directions, too.

LARRY

And you'll continue to tell the story of Passover.

JERRY

Just as G-d intended.

LARRY

While laughing at our sitcom.

JERRY

Just as G-d also intended.

PASSOVER

INT. COMEDY CLUB - NIGHT

JERRY

Do you know why they call it Passover? G-d told
Moses that the Israelites should mark their
doorposts with lamb's blood. So that He could "pass
over" their houses. And spare them from the plague
of the killing of the first born. My question is: Who
was put in charge of telling everyone? That's a big
job. There's a lot counting on that job. What if
someone isn't home? How did they tell them? Did
they leave a note? Probably not. The Egyptians
could see it. Would have ruined the whole plan. Did
they just take the liberty of putting lamb's blood on
the door? What about when that family gets home,
sees blood all over their door? "Honey, do you see
this? Someone put blood on our door. Someone's
out to get us! You better get off the couch and wipe
this off." "I'm busy! Have our first born do it!"

SEDER

INT. THE COFFEE SHOP - DAY

JERRY AND GEORGE ARE IN THE BOOTH.
GEORGE IS BEGGING JERRY FOR SOMETHING.

GEORGE
Jerry, come on.

JERRY
No, George. You can't have a Seder at my house.

GEORGE
Why not?!

JERRY
Do you know what food makes the most crumbs in
the known universe? Matzo! If you have a Seder, I'll
never be able to get those crumbs out of my carpet!

GEORGE

We'll do the Seder without matzo then.

JERRY

Do the Seder without matzo? Would you listen to
yourself? There's no Passover story without matzo.
That'd be like the Superman story without
kryptonite. It'd make no sense. You don't know
anything about Passover. What are you even doing
this for?

GEORGE

I met an Israeli woman, Jerry.

JERRY

Of course you did.

GEORGE

Do you know how beautiful Sephardic women are?
I've always had a thing for Sephardic women.

JERRY

Is there any type of woman you haven't always had
a thing for?

GEORGE

None. I have a thing for every woman.

JERRY

They just never want any<u>thing</u> to do with you.

GEORGE

Exactly, Jerry! That's what's so beautiful about this
situation with the Israeli woman. She said she has
nowhere to spend the holiday. I told her we always
have Seder at your house. I told her, come to Seder
at your house.

JERRY

Wait. You already invited her to Seder at my
house?!

ELAINE ENTERS AND SITS NEXT TO GEORGE.

ELAINE

What's a Seder?

GEORGE

It's, like, Jewish Thanksgiving.

ELAINE

I love Thanksgiving! Why wasn't I invited?

JERRY

Because it's not happening!

ELAINE

You sure about that? I've been looking for
something to do this weekend. I met this
entrepreneur bigwig, Ramses. He's considering
investing in my very own publishing press. Can you
guys believe that? I'd have my very own publishing
press. No more working for crazy bosses! No more
craziness in my life!! No more crazy!!!

GEORGE

You sure about that?

JERRY

Sorry, folks, Seder's not happening.

ELAINE

Come on, Jerry, this would be perfect. I need to wine and dine this guy, but on a budget, but without it looking like it's on a budget. So this traditional, no frills, Jewish Thanksgiving, or whatever it is. It's perfect.

GEORGE

What makes you think it won't have frills? Because I'm throwing it? There'll be frills.

ELAINE

You don't know how to frill, George.

GEORGE

Oh, I can frill, baby. George knows how to frill.

JERRY

Name one time you frilled, Liberace.

GEORGE

My wedding. My wedding was going to have frills.

ELAINE

The wedding you didn't have, because your fiancée
died, licking your no-frills envelopes?

JERRY

Do you see the irony? If you had frilled, you'd be a
married man. Unhappily married. But married
nonetheless. If you had frilled. Or could frill.

GEORGE

You're right. I better find someone who can frill this
Seder for me.

JERRY

You know who is all frills?

KRAMER ENTERS THE COFFEE SHOP. YOUR
SEDER TABLE CLAPS. HE SITS NEXT TO JERRY.
BUT HE LACKS HIS USUAL LUSTER TODAY.

JERRY

What's with you?

KRAMER

You know my friend, Bob Sacamano?

ELAINE

Not really. I mean, we've heard you talk about him
for years. But we've never met him. Does he really
exist?

KRAMER

Oh, he exists. Though I wish he didn't right now.
Because he just pulled the plug on our Easter egg
hunt business.

JERRY

What was that billion dollar idea?

KRAMER

We were going to start an upscale Easter egg hunt
business. Called The Nor'Easter. Where you
scavenger hunt The North Eastern Seaboard from
Good Friday to Easter Sunday, looking for eggs.

ELAINE

So what happened?

KRAMER

Bob Sacamano's egg guy couldn't source enough
eggs. The chickens are on strike. Can you believe
that? I offered to sic my rooster, you know, Lil'
Jerry, on them. But that's against regulations. And
there's no way we're doing plastic eggs with candy
inside. Or chocolate eggs with cream in the middle.
None of that ersatz Easter. I'm devastated. I feel
dead inside. Dead. Like I got nothing to live for. No
hope. No faith. I got nothing!

GEORGE

This is great!

KRAMER

What? What do you mean, "This is great?"

GEORGE

Now you can do something for Passover.

KRAMER

Passover? What's there to do for Passover?

GEORGE

Tons of stuff. There's the wine. The Haggadah book.
The Seder plate. The pillows. The songs. The matzo,
of course. Plenty to work with.

KRAMER

I like the sound of all that. Count me in!

GEORGE

Great. You can use my Seder at Jerry's for your trial
run. Just remember. Don't skimp on the frills.

KRAMER

Oh, Bubala! I can feel my insides filling back up with hope again. I'm breathing that sweet, sweet air of faith again.

JERRY

Now hold on a minute. I told you all, no Seder at my house!

KRAMER

What?! Come on, Jerry. Get in touch with your roots. Tap into your faith. You think the man upstairs isn't judging this decision as we speak?

ELAINE

Please, Jerry? We're talking about my very own publishing press here?

GEORGE

A Sephardic woman, Jerry?! A Sephardi?!

JERRY

Oh alright!

THE REMOVAL OF THE HAMETZ

INT. JERRY'S APARTMENT - DAY

JERRY OPENS THE DOOR TO HIS APARTMENT.
IT HAS BEEN TORN APART. A PILE OF FOOD
BURNS ON THE GROUND.

JERRY

What on G-d's green earth?

JERRY RUNS TO THE SINK. HE POURS A CUP
OF WATER.

JERRY

I can't believe this.

KRAMER ENTERS THE APARTMENT, SEES
JERRY PUTTING OUT THE FIRE.

KRAMER

What are you doing?! Don't put that out!

JERRY

What am *I* doing?! What is this?!

KRAMER

It's hametz. I'm burning the hametz!

KRAMER PICKS UP THE SOGGY REMAINS OF
THE HALF-BURNT PILE.

KRAMER

And you ruined it!

JERRY

What's hametz? And why are you burning it in my
apartment?!

KRAMER

Hametz is anything leavened with yeast in your
house, Jerry. For Passover, you're supposed to
search, collect, and burn it all. Before nightfall.

JERRY PICKS UP A CHARRED BOX.

JERRY

Did you burn my cereal boxes, too?

KRAMER

Yep, cereal's leavened. At least I think it is. Not 100
percent sure. There are a few different rabbinical
interpretations. Anyway. It's all gone.

JERRY

I had an original Lou Gehrig Wheaties box from
1934! Kramer, how could you?!

KRAMER STAMMERS AND STAGGERS.

JERRY

This Seder's already ruined my apartment and my
irreplaceable memorabilia, and it hasn't even
started yet?!

KRAMER

Maybe if we say the prayer you'll feel better.

<u>EVERYONE:</u>

בָּרוּךְ אַתָּה יהוה אֱלֹהֵינוּ מֶלֶךְ
הָעוֹלָם, אֲשֶׁר קִדְּשָׁנוּ בְּמִצְוֹתָיו, וְצִוָּנוּ
עַל בְּעוּר חָמֵץ.

Baruch atah Adonai, Eloheinu Melech ha'olam,
asher kid'shanu b'mitzvotav v'tzivanu al biur
hametz.

Praised Are You, Our G-d, who blesses us with
mitzvot and instructs us to remove hametz.

KRAMER
Tell you what. You go down to the coffee shop. I'll
finish setting up. Come back at sundown. Your
apartment will be as good as new. Better than new.

JERRY
It can't get any worse than this.

THE YOM TOV CANDLE LIGHTING

INT. JERRY'S APARTMENT - EVENING

JERRY ENTERS HIS APARTMENT TO FIND IT
OVERFLOWING WITH PEOPLE. KRAMER AND
GEORGE ARE THERE, AS WELL AS GEORGE'S
ISRAELI LOVE INTEREST, YAEL, AND
GEORGE'S PARENTS, ESTELLE AND FRANK.

GEORGE RUSHES OVER TO JERRY.

GEORGE

Can you believe this, Jerry? Kramer told my parents
I was throwing a Seder. Of course they demanded
to come. And now the Sephardic girl Yael's here,
too. What am I going to do? There's no way I can
look attractive to a woman in front of my parents.
Not a chance!

JERRY

Some might say it's because of them that you can't
look attractive to a woman in general.

YAEL JOINS JERRY AND GEORGE.

YAEL

Hi. Is this Jerry?

GEORGE

Yeah. Yael, this is Jerry. Jerry, this is Yael.

JERRY

Yaello.

YAEL

Thank you for inviting us into your home, Jerry. It's
a true mitzvah to open your home for a Seder.

JERRY

You can thank your friend, Georgiah-Yitzhak here,
not me.

YAEL

What a beautiful Hebrew name, Georgiah-Yitzhak.

GEORGE GIVES JERRY STINK-EYE FOR GIVING
HIM THE FAKE HEBREW NICKNAME.

GEORGE

Thank you.

FRANK AND ESTELLE APPROACH.

ESTELLE

You have a Hebrew name now? He refused to have
a Bar Mitzvah and now he's hosting Seders with a
Hebrew name. What's going on here?

YAEL

You didn't have a Bar Mitzvah?

GEORGE

I, uh, got laryngitis and lost my voice. Terrible
thing. Tragic.

ESTELLE

No, you didn't. What are you talking about?

GEORGE

Yes, I did. You just don't remember.

(to Yael)

I could still have a Bar Mitzvah though? Maybe I
still should? Would you want me to?

YAEL

Oh, yes, you absolutely must. Bar Mitzvahs are not
just a metaphorical milestone, they're essential to
becoming a self-actualized adult.

JERRY

This might explain everything?

FRANK

I'm not paying for it.

KRAMER IS HAVING TROUBLE GETTING THE
YOM TOV CANDLES INTO THE HOLDERS.

YAEL NOTICES.

YAEL

Excuse me.

SHE CROSSES TO HELP KRAMER.

ESTELLE

Who is she, George? Is she your girlfriend?

GEORGE

No. She's not my girlfriend, Ma. She's nobody.

ESTELLE

She's nobody?

GEORGE

She's a person. A person I met. That I invited here.

ESTELLE

A person. A person you met? What kind of a person
talks about another person like that? "A person. A
person I met?"

FRANK

Not the person I raised.

KRAMER

Alright, everybody, sit down. Sun sets in...

KRAMER CHECKS HIS WATCH WRIST, WHICH
HAS NO WATCH ON IT.

KRAMER

One minute from now. Oy vey! We gotta get started.

JERRY

What about Elaine?

KRAMER PUTS HIS HAND UP.

KRAMER

Ahhhhh! No time!

EVERYONE SITS DOWN AT THE TABLE.

KRAMER

According to Jewish law, the woman of the house is
supposed to light the candles. But since Jerry has
no woman, and likely never will, because he fixates
on every little, insignificant, superficial flaw. And
because this very nice, very beautiful woman, Yael,
helped me set the candles, let's have her light 'em.

ESTELLE

What?! Why does she get to light the candles?

GEORGE

Ma.

ESTELLE

She's the woman of the house now? You said she
was nobody.

GEORGE

Ma, sheket!

ESTELLE

Just a person you said. Just a person you met.

31

GEORGE

Sheket, Ma, sheket now!

FRANK

You let your mother light the candles at your Seder,
George, or we're walking out. We'll walk out! It'll be
a walkout!

GEORGE

Go ahead, walk out! G-d let it be a walkout! I don't
want you here! You weren't even invited!

JERRY

Well, this is off to a great start.

YAEL

Georgiah-Yitzhak, what's gotten into you? Your
parents are right. Thank you for your generous
offer, Kramer. But it must be Georgiah-Yitzhak's
mother's honor to light the Yom Tov Candles. Not
mine. Estelle, please.

ESTELLE

I like her, George.

FRANK

Yeah, you should make her more than a person.

ESTELLE

Now how does this prayer go?

<u>EVERYONE:</u>

בָּרוּךְ אַתָּה אֲדֹנָי אֱלֹהֵינוּ מֶלֶךְ
הָעוֹלָם אֲשֶׁר קִדְּשָׁנוּ בְּמִצְוֹתָיו וְצִוָּנוּ
לְהַדְלִיק נֵר שֶׁל [שַׁבָּת וְשֶׁל] יוֹם טוֹ

Baruch atah Adonai, Eloheinu Melech ha'olam,
asher kid'shanu b'mitzvotav v'tzivanu l'hadlik ner
shel Yom Tov.

Praised Are You, Our G-d, who blesses us with
mitzvot and instructs us to ignite the lights of the
festival day.

THE SEDER TABLE

AS ESTELLE LIGHTS THE CANDLES, FRANK
SURVEYS THE SEDER TABLE AND REMARKS:

FRANK

Who set this Seder Table?

KRAMER

I did.

FRANK

Well, it's all wrong.

KRAMER

What do you mean? What's wrong with it, Frank? I
got the pillows and cushions all set up for reclining.
With levels. Levels. Like they had back then with
the Egyptians. And I have the three matzo.

FRANK POKES KRAMER'S MATZO, WHICH IS
ODDLY FLUFFY.

FRANK

You call this matzo?

KRAMER

No, I call it, "Matzo, Not So?!" It's matzo that tastes
so much like bread it can't possibly be matzo. I
made it myself. It's my next million-dollar idea.

FRANK

That'll never sell.

SUDDENLY, ELAINE ENTERS WITH A DASHING
MIDDLE-EASTERN MAN, RAMSES.

ELAINE

Say dere, this the Seder?

JERRY

That's what they say, dear.

ELAINE

Everyone, this is Ramses. Ramses, this is everyone.
He's an entrepreneur visiting from—

RAMSES WAVES. HE HAS A THICK ACCENT.

RAMSES

Alexandria, Egypt.

GEORGE SPIT-TAKES SOME WATER.

ESTELLE

Did he say Egypt?

GEORGE

He said Virginia. He's visiting from Alexandria,
Virginia.

RAMSES

My first Seder. What's all this on this decorative
plate?

KRAMER

I'm glad you asked. We have to describe each item.

Here, we have the Zeroa. Supposed to be a broiled

lamb shank. But I don't have an oven right now. So

I took home some Kenny Rogers chicken.

Love Kenny. Also hate Kenny.

(wistful)

Kenny...

FRANK

What's that?

KRAMER

That's the Betzah. A hard-boiled egg.

ESTELLE

Why are the words "Welcome to Boston" painted on

it in pink and green?

JERRY

Ah, the Nor'Easter lives on.

RAMSES

What about this dip?

KRAMER

Maror. Horseradish.

RAMSES

And this dip?

KRAMER

Chazeret. More horseradish.

RAMSES

Two of the same kind of dip? Fascinating.

YAEL

The Charoset looks divine.

KRAMER

It is. My own recipe. A sweet mixture of fruits, nuts,
and wine. Joe's cantaloupe, Snickers nougat, and
Hennigan's scotch.

JERRY

Divine.

ELAINE

Is that a Big Salad?

KRAMER

The Karpas. Parsley or any green vegetable.

Including a Big Salad. Dressed, of course, with salt

water.

RAMSES

What's this extra plate and wine goblet for? Are we

expecting another guest?

KRAMER

Yeah, Newman might drop by.

JERRY

(shakes his fist)

Newman.

39

RAMSES
Who is this Newman?

KRAMER
Our neighbor. First name's actually Elijah. Who
would have guessed? He might announce the
arrival of the Messiah.

JERRY
If he delivers the news anything like he delivers
mail, no one will ever know.

ESTELLE
What's this orange doing on the Seder plate? I don't
remember oranges at my parents' Seders?

GEORGE
I'm glad you asked, Ma. It's actually a modern
invention symbolizing the inclusion of women. It's
for forward-thinking, feminist Jews—

GEORGE IS INTERRUPTED BY YAEL.

YAEL

Who my Orthodox parents said I should never
Seder with.

GEORGE

Same with mine!

GEORGE PICKS UP THE ORANGE AND THROWS
IT IN JERRY'S BATHROOM. YAEL SMILES.

ELAINE

When do we eat? Is this all we're eating? I'm
starving.

KRAMER

Eat? We can't eat until we finish reading the
Haggadah.

ELAINE

How long does that take?

KRAMER

Hours!

JERRY

And it is bo-ring!

ELAINE

Dear G-d. Is there anything to drink at least?

THE FIRST CUP OF WINE

KRAMER HANDS ELAINE A BOTTLE OF
MANISCHEWITZ WINE.

KRAMER
It's actually time for the first cup of wine.

ELAINE
Yes, wine. Thank G-d.

JERRY
I wouldn't call that wine.

ELAINE
It's not wine?

ESTELLE
It's wine.

JERRY
It's not wine.

FRANK EXAMINES THE BOTTLE.

FRANK

It says wine.

JERRY

It's barely even a beverage. Unless you enjoy the
flavor of children's cough syrup.

ELAINE

(sarcastic)

Perfect.

RAMSES TAKES A GLASS AND DOWNS IT.
EVERYONE STARES AT HIM, CURIOUSLY.

RAMSES

What? I like it. It tastes like grape juice. I love this
Jewish Thanksgiving! I see a bright future for the
two of us, Elaine.

ELAINE
You do?

RAMSES
I do.

ELAINE
You hear that, Jerry? That calls for another glass!

ELAINE POURS A GENEROUS GLASS FOR
RAMSES. THEN SLIGHTLY LESS GENEROUS
GLASSES FOR JERRY AND KRAMER, AND EVEN
LESS GENEROUS FOR GEORGE AND YAEL, AND
WAY LESS FOR GEORGE'S PARENTS.

<u>EVERYONE:</u>

בָּרוּךְ אַתָּה ה', אֱ-לֹהֵינוּ מֶלֶךְ
הָעוֹלָם, בּוֹרֵא פְּרִי הַגָּפֶן.

Baruch atah Adonai, Eloheinu Melech ha'olam,
bo're p'ri hagafen.

Praised Are You, Our G-d, who creates the fruit of
the vine.

THE SHEHECHEYANU

INT. COMEDY CLUB - NIGHT

JERRY

We say the Shehecheyanu to give thanks to G-d for enabling us to reach this moment in our lives. My question is: Do you thank G-d for every moment in life? What about that moment in life when you're stuck in traffic on the Long Island Expressway and someone rear-ends you? Do you thank G-d for enabling you to reach that moment in life? And what about that moment after you've been stuck in traffic and were rear-ended, when you get to the airport and learn that you missed your flight and you now have to take the last seat available on the plane, and it's next to the bathroom? And what about the moment after those two moments when you miss the show you booked and went on the plane and drove to the airport for? Shehech is up with all that?

EVERYONE:

בָּרוּךְ אַתָּה יְיָ אֱלֹהֵינוּ מֶלֶךְ
הָעוֹלָם שֶׁהֶחֱיָנוּ וְקִיְּמָנוּ
וְהִגִּיעָנוּ לַזְּמַן הַזֶּה:

Baruch atah Adonai, Eloheinu Melech ha'olam,
shehecheyanu v'ki'manu v'higi-anu laz'man hazeh.

Praised Are You, G-d, who has sustained us,
maintained us, and enabled us to reach this
moment in life.

THE URCHATZ

INT. JERRY'S APARTMENT - NIGHT

ELAINE
Now what?

KRAMER
It's time for the Urchatz. Where we all wash our
hands before the meal with this.

KRAMER PASSES A BOWL FILLED WITH
WATER TO ELAINE.

ELAINE
OK...

ELAINE WASHES HER HANDS. THEN WHEN
SHE IS DIRECTED BY KRAMER TO PASS THE
BOWL TO RAMSES, JERRY REALIZES WHAT'S
GOING ON. HE TURNS HORRIFIED:

49

JERRY

Wait. We're all washing our hands with the same
bowl of water. That's—that's crazy! It defeats the
whole purpose of washing your hands! Washing
them with the filth of other people's hands? Why
even wash your hands if you're going to wash your
hands like that?!

YAEL FINISHES WASHING HER HANDS. SHE
PASSES THE BOWL TO GEORGE. EVEN
THOUGH THE BOWL HAS BEEN USED BY
ELAINE, RAMSES, GEORGE'S PARENTS, AND
KRAMER, GEORGE GLEEFULLY WASHES HIS
HANDS IN THE WATER FOR YAEL'S BENEFIT.

GEORGE

I don't mind one bit. I find it revitalizing,
refreshing, and completely sanitary.

GEORGE PASSES THE BOWL TO JERRY.

GEORGE

Jerry?

JERRY

No, thanks.

YAEL

But, Jerry, you must.

JERRY

I'm good.

YAEL LOOKS VERY DISAPPOINTED.

YAEL

You're the only one at the table who hasn't. And
you're the host!

GEORGE NOTICES HIS LOVE INTEREST'S
SEVERE DISAPPOINTMENT. HE RE-EXTENDS
THE BOWL TO JERRY.

GEORGE

Jerry. Take it. Wash your hands.

JERRY

Nuh-uh.

ELAINE

Go ahead, Jer. I did it. First. But still.

JERRY SHAKES HIS HEAD NO.

GEORGE

Wash your hands, Jerry!

JERRY VEHEMENTLY SHAKES HIS HEAD NO.

GEORGE GRABS JERRY'S HANDS AND DUNKS
THEM IN THE WATER. JERRY MAKES A
COMPLETELY DISGUSTED FACE. BUT YAEL
LOOKS HAPPY. GEORGE NOTICES, FEELS
JUSTIFIED. HE RELEASES JERRY'S HANDS.
JERRY STARES AT HIS RUINED HANDS.

THE KARPAS

ELAINE

Now do we eat? I'm starving.

KRAMER

Sort of. Next up is the Karpas. Who wants to do the
Karpas? Yael?

YAEL

I'd be honored. For the Karpas, we dip fresh green
vegetables into bitter, salty water. It symbolizes the
celebration of a painful moment in Jewish history,
by combining a metaphor of tears and slavery, the
salt water, with one of spring and rebirth, the green
vegetable.

YAEL DIPS SOME OF THE BIG SALAD INTO THE
SALT WATER. SHE BITES THE VEGETABLE.

YAEL

Mmm.

YAEL PASSES THE KARPAS TO GEORGE. HE
TAKES THE BIG SALAD AND SALT WATER
NEXT, DIPS, AND BITES.

GEORGE
Mmm.

YAEL SMILES. HOWEVER, GEORGE THEN
RE-DIPS THE BITTEN VEGETABLE INTO THE
SALT WATER AND TAKES ANOTHER BITE.

GEORGE
Mmmmmmm.

YAEL LOOKS AT GEORGE. SHE'S DISGUSTED.

YAEL
What are you doing?

GEORGE
What?

YAEL

You just double dipped the Karpas?

GEORGE

Excuse me?

YAEL

You dipped the Karpas. Bit it. And dipped it again.

GEORGE

So?

FRANK

It's like putting your whole mouth in the Karpas,

George!

GEORGE

I didn't get enough salt water the first time. I like to
really feel the tears of our people. Is that so bad?

YAEL

There's no double dipping. In general. Of anything.

ESTELLE

Who raised you to double dip? We didn't raise him
to double dip. I can tell you that.

FRANK

I'm sorry you had to see that, Yael.

GEORGE

Can we just say the prayer already?!

YAEL

Georgiah-Yitzhak, you and your parents remind me
exactly of my parents and my brother, Mordecai.
The way they hector you, the way you quarrel, the
way they berate you, the way you fight.

GEORGE
(unsure)
Yeah?

YAEL

It's the way of love.

56

YAEL PECKS GEORGE ON THE CHEEK. GEORGE
LIGHTS UP.

JERRY

Alrighty. Should we say the prayer?

<u>EVERYONE:</u>

בָּרוּךְ אַתָּה ה' אֱ-לֹהֵינוּ מֶלֶךְ
הָעוֹלָם בּוֹרֵא פְּרִי הָאֲדָמָה.

*Baruch atah Adonai Eloheinu Melech ha`olam,
bo'rei p'ri ha'adama.*

*Praised Are You, Our G-d, who creates the fruit of
the earth.*

THE YAHATZ

GEORGE TALKS TO JERRY IN THE KITCHEN
BETWEEN SECTIONS IN THE SEDER.

GEORGE

Can you believe this, Jerry? The more my parents
infantilize and humiliate and emasculate me—

JERRY

The more Yael likes you.

GEORGE

For my whole life, the formative interactions with
my Jewish mother and Italian father have
sabotaged any chance I've had at happiness in a
romantic relationship.

JERRY

But meeting a woman who was raised in an
analogous environment, with overbearing and
bickering and unhappy parents—

58

GEORGE

Means she can love me, the real, miserable me.

JERRY

What are you going to do?

ESTELLE

George! What are you doing over there? Sit down
already! We have so much more to go!

GEORGE

(sotto)

I'll play the part, Jerry, I'll play the part.

FRANK

George! Sit! Down! It's time for the Yahatz! The
breaking of the middle matzo!

GEORGE

(yelling, dramatically, for effect)

ALRIGHT, ALRIGHT! I'M COMING! GET OFF MY
BACK!

YAEL SMILES IN DELIGHT.

KRAMER

The Jewish people eat matzo in memory of the flight of their ancestors, who as slaves faced many false starts before they were allowed to leave Egypt. When they finally had the chance, they grabbed whatever sustenance they had and fled, even if it wasn't fully baked. However, it is a common misconception that the unleavened matzo they ate then is the dry, unsavory, practically inedible cardboard we eat now. Big Matzo companies have mass-produced the matzo into an abomination our ancestors would never have recognized, let alone eat. Today, I bring you the real thing, the kosher for Passover: "Matzo, Not So?!"

KRAMER WHIPS OFF THE MATZO COVER TO REVEAL THE THREE PUFFY MATZOS.

RAMSES
Wow!

JERRY

Kramer, are you sure that bread's not leavened?

KRAMER

Jerry. It's unleavened heaven. There's absolutely no yeast. Now someone take the middle "Matzo, Not So?!" and break it into two pieces for the Yahatz.

RAMSES

May I have the honor?

KRAMER

Gimmel up!

RAMSES TAKES THE MIDDLE "MATZO, NOT SO?!" AND RIPS THE PUFFY MATZO INTO TWO.

THE AFIKOMEN

RAMSES GULPS WINE, GETTING TIPSY. HE
TAKES A BITE OF THE RIPPED MATZO.

RAMSES
This is delicious. It's like the baladi bread I have
back home in Alexandria.

YAEL FROWNS.

GEORGE
You're not supposed to eat it yet, Ramses.

ELAINE
He can eat anything, anytime he wants,
Georgey-Yitzhak.

GEORGE
Not really. We're supposed to hide the bigger half,
the Afikomen, so that the youngest guests can
search for it and win a cash prize.

RAMSES

I'd like to give out a cash prize!

JERRY

Now this is getting fun.

ELAINE

Ramses, you don't have to do that.

RAMSES

No, I want to, Elaine.

RAMSES PRODUCES A CHECKBOOK. ELAINE
THINKS SHE CATCHES RAMSES' DRIFT.

ELAINE

Oh! OK!

I'm so glad the generous spirit of this wonderful
holiday is moving you, Ramses. It means so much
to me that you're going to invest in—

RAMSES HANDS KRAMER A CHECK.

RAMSES

Kramer, I'd like to invest five million dollars in your
bread business.

ELAINE

GET OUT!

ELAINE PUSHES RAMSES.

RAMSES

You want me to leave?

KRAMER

Of course not. She just does that whenever she gets
excited. That's quite an offer, Ramses. I'll take it!

KRAMER TAKES THE CHECK FROM RAMSES.
ELAINE LOOKS FURIOUS, BUT SWALLOWS
HER PRIDE. AS RAMSES PUTS HIS CHECKBOOK
BACK IN HIS JACKET, ELAINE STOPS HIM.

64

ELAINE

Let's keep that out, shall we. Who knows when the
mood to give out more cash prizes might strike?
And let's have another glass of wine!

ELAINE POURS RAMSES ANOTHER HUGE
GLASS OF WINE.

THE FOUR QUESTIONS

THERE'S A KNOCK ON THE DOOR.

JERRY

Who could that be?

JERRY OPENS THE DOOR.

JERRY

Yeah?

UNCLE LEO

Yeah? Is that how you greet your Uncle Leo?!

JERRY

Hi, Uncle Leo.

UNCLE LEO

You're having a Seder, and you forgot about your
Uncle Leo?

JERRY

It's not really my Seder, Uncle Leo.

UNCLE LEO

Why is this night different from all other nights? It doesn't seem to be different to your Uncle Leo, he gets snubbed like usual.

JERRY

You didn't tell my parents that I was having a Seder, did you, Uncle—

JERRY'S PARENTS, MORTY AND HELEN, ENTER CARRYING SUITCASES.

MORTY

Jerry!

JERRY

Mom, Dad, no! You guys flew all the way from Florida for this?

67

HELEN

We wouldn't miss your Seder for the world.

MORTY

Where are we in the Seder, where did you guys
leave off?

MORTY AND HELEN NOTICE FRANK AND
ESTELLE AT THE TABLE. THEY TURN COLD.

HELEN

Oh, hello, Costanzas.

MORTY

Maybe we'll go to the hotel first and unpack.

FRANK

Why? Because we're here?! You can't stand to be at
the same Seder as us?!

ESTELLE

You still don't care for us, do you, Seinfelds?

HELEN

No, no, we care for you. It's just such a long flight.

MORTY

And there are two nights of these Seders, right?

(quiet, to Jerry)

Are they going to be here for both nights?

JERRY

There's not going to be two nights of this at my
house, I'll tell you that right now! Come on, you
flew all the way from Florida, sit down.

HELEN

Oh alright.

KRAMER

You can pick up with the four questions.

Why is this night different from all other nights?

MORTY

OK. I know those. On all other nights we may eat
hametz and matzo, but on this night, only matzo.

HELEN

On all other nights we eat many vegetables, but on
this night, only maror.

MORTY

On all other nights, we eat either sitting up or
reclining, but on this night, we recline.

HELEN

On all other nights, we don't dip even once, but on
this night, we dip twice.

GEORGE LEAPS UP FROM HIS CHAIR.

GEORGE

Ah-ha! See! You dip twice! You double dip, baby!

FRANK

That can't be right.

YAEL

It just means there are two separate dippings.

ESTELLE

You know who would know, Lloyd Braun.

KRAMER

I invited him, too. I wonder where he is?

SUDDENLY THE DOOR OPENS. IT'S:

ESTELLE

Lloyd!

LLOYD ENTERS. FRANK SHAKES HIS HAND.

YAEL

Who is this guy?

GEORGE

I grew up with him. He's the son my parents wish
they had. Seeing the way they fawn over him, it's
extremely demoralizing!

GEORGE NOTICES YAEL'S EYES WIDEN IN
EXCITEMENT.

YAEL
(into it)
That sounds terrible.

GEORGE
(catching on; milking it)
Oh, it is, Yael. It is.

THE FOUR CHILDREN

FRANK AND ESTELLE SHOVE GEORGE OUT OF
THE WAY TO GIVE LLOYD GEORGE'S SEAT.
LLOYD SITS DOWN.

FRANK

Perfect timing, Lloyd. It's time for the Four
Children. I almost made the Four Children part of
my Festivus holiday because I liked the criticism of
the children so much. Suffice it to say, I already
have my speech planned. Here goes. The Wise Child
is the better child. The Child everyone wishes they
had instead of their own. He is the Lloyd Braun.

ESTELLE

Good for you, Lloyd!

GEORGE WINCES. BUT THEN NOTICES YAEL
SMILING AT HIM.

FRANK

Lloyd, as the Wise Child, I instruct you to say...

LLOYD BRAUN

"What are the testimonials, statutes, and laws
commanded of us?"

ESTELLE

Very good, Lloyd!

GEORGE WINCES EVEN MORE. HE LOOKS
BETWEEN LLOYD AND YAEL, NOT SURE HOW
MUCH MORE OF HIS PARENTS' FAWNING HE
CAN TAKE.

FRANK

The Wicked Child is the disappointment of the
family. The child the family wishes they didn't have.
The deceitful and duplicitous one. He is the George.
George, even though you hosted this Seder, you put
an orange on the table and you didn't want your
mother to light the candles. You exclude and you
rebel. You're *wicked!* So you say...

FRANK MOTIONS TO GEORGE. GEORGE IS
NOW IRATE; HE DOESN'T WANT TO SAY IT.
BUT YAEL URGES HIM ON.

GEORGE
(quietly)
"What does this worship mean to you?"

FRANK
Implying it doesn't concern you, so we tell you:

ESTELLE
"I do this worship because G-d labored on my
behalf by taking me out of Egypt."

FRANK
And then we blunt your teeth.

FRANK WHACKS GEORGE IN THE TEETH.

GEORGE
Ow, watch it!

YAEL

I wonder who the Simple Child is?

SHE SLYLY GRINS.

FRANK

The Simple Child is easily overwhelmed. He's short,
stocky, slow-witted, and bald. He is also George.

GEORGE STEAMS.

FRANK

From now on, for your own good, you should only
be capable of asking, "What's this?"

FRANK MOTIONS TO GEORGE.

GEORGE
(stewing)
What's this?

FRANK

We tell you...

ESTELLE

"With a strong hand G-d took us out of Egypt."

GEORGE

If you blunt my teeth again—

FRANK

Uh-uh-uh. You can only say, "What's this?"

FRANK MOTIONS FOR GEORGE TO SAY IT.
GEORGE LOOKS OVER AT EAGER YAEL.

GEORGE
(barely audible)
What's this?

YAEL PUTS HER ARM AROUND GEORGE.
GEORGE MOMENTARILY BRIGHTENS.

FRANK

And, of course, there is the Child Too Young To Ask.

JERRY

Don't tell me.

FRANK

Yes, George is also the Child Too Young To Ask. At least, he acts that way. He acts like an immature, undeveloped, completely inadequate, and practically disabled child—

GEORGE CAN'T TAKE IT ANYMORE. HE PULLS YAEL'S ARM OFF AND STANDS UP.

GEORGE

Enough! Enough humiliating George in front of everyone all the time! George has had enough! George wants you gone! George wants you to leave right now! Get out! Get out! Get out!

ESTELLE

If that's how you really feel.

FRANK

We'll go.

FRANK AND ESTELLE STAND UP, LOOK SAD.
YAEL LOOKS UPSET, TOO.

YAEL

Then I'm leaving, too.

George

So be it.

GEORGE LETS YAEL AND HIS PARENTS LEAVE.

JERRY

Wow, George, you're letting the Sephardi go?

GEORGE IMMEDIATELY REGRETS HIS CHOICE.

GEORGE

I know! What am I doing? What a time to develop a
backbone?!

GEORGE OPENS THE WINDOW, CALLS OUT.

GEORGE

Yael, wait!

GEORGE RACES OUT THE DOOR AFTER THEM.

THE MAGID

RAMSES

Very strange man.

KRAMER

Indeed. Next up is a favorite part of Seders, perhaps
the highlight. Who wants to do The Magid—

ELAINE

Me! I will.

ELAINE SMILES AT RAMSES, EAGER TO
IMPRESS.

KRAMER

OK!

ELAINE

What do I do?

KRAMER

Read from this section of the Haggadah.

KRAMER SHOWS ELAINE THE PAGE TO READ.

ELAINE

Many years ago, the evil Egyptians—

RAMSES

The evil Egyptians?

ELAINE

That can't be right?

KRAMER

What? Everyone knows the evil Egyptians led by
their evil Pharaoh, they enslaved the Jews.

RAMSES

We did not!

KRAMER

Did, too.

82

RAMSES

Who says?

KRAMER

The Torah. And Charlton Heston.

RAMSES

What does the Torah say exactly?

KRAMER

That the Pharaoh refused to let the leader of the

Jews, Moses, and his people leave, so G-d sent

down ten plagues that vanquished the Egyptians.

RAMSES

What?! What plagues?

KRAMER

Everyone say them with me, while dropping a drop

of wine from your cup onto your plate.

EVERYONE:

DAM, turning their water into blood; TZFARDEAH, releasing frogs on them; KINIM, lice; AROV, wild beasts; DEVER, diseasing their livestock; SH'HIN, boils; BARAD, hail; ARBEH, locusts; HOSHEKH, darkness for three days; and finally, MAKAT B'KHOROT, the killing of their firstborns.

RAMSES

Your people did all that to my people?!

ELAINE

Can you really trust everything you read these days?

RAMSES

You take it back and apologize or I'll take back my 5 million dollars, Kramer. And I'll also take back the 5 million dollars I was going to give Elaine to start her own publishing press. I'll pass on both your deals!

ELAINE

Kramer! You take it back and apologize right now!

KRAMER

No can do!

ELAINE

Kramer!

KRAMER

It's a hard no, Pharaoh!

RAMSES

Then it's a hard pass! I'm <u>passing over</u> both your

deals!

ELAINE

No! Ramses, no!

RAMSES GRABS THE CHECK FROM KRAMER
AND TEARS IT IN TWO.

RAMSES

I'm going to tell all my rich friends about this,
Elaine. You'll never get your own publishing press.
Never!

ELAINE

Oh, please don't.

RAMSES EXITS. KRAMER SLAMS THE DOOR:

KRAMER

What a schmuck!

ELAINE

I can't believe this!

KRAMER

I can. There are always guys like that in every
episode of our peoples' lives. That's why we say:

EVERYONE:

Not only one enemy has risen against us, but in every generation there are those who will rise against us. G-d promised to deliver us from those who seek us harm. G-d will deliver us as He did in Egypt, with a mighty hand and an outstretched arm, with awesome spectacle, and miraculous signs and wonders.

THE MIRIAM CUP

ELAINE

Can this night get any worse? And I am so hungry.
Are we ever going to eat? Should we just order
some Chinese?!

KRAMER

No! Now we do another cup of wine just for the
women, called the Miriam Cup, which symbolizes
the help of Moses' sister, Miriam, and other Jewish
women.

ELAINE POURS HERSELF A HUGE GLASS.

ELAINE

Might as well drink my dinner if no one's serving it.

ELAINE DOWNS THE MIRIAM CUP. WOMEN AT
YOUR SEDER FEEL FREE TO DO THE SAME.

DAYEINU

INT. COMEDY CLUB - NIGHT

JERRY

I think of Dayeinu as the song of the Jewish
mother. You come home to visit a Jewish mother,
she not only picks you up from the airport during a
snowstorm, she also cooks you a huge meal. You'll
say, "It's enough just to get together. You didn't
have to do all this." And what does the Jewish
mother do, she plies you with dessert. It's enough,
we say, Dayeinu. But she hears that and gives you
another scoop of ice cream. It's the same with the
Jews and G-d. G-d not only slays the Egyptians'
firstborns, He also gives us all their wealth. It's
enough, we say, Dayeinu. But G-d hears that, He
splits the sea for us. It's enough, Dayeinu, already.
G-d goes ahead and drowns our oppressors in the
sea. And on and on until He, the original Jewish
mother, brings us into the Land of Israel. Dayeinu!

THE SECOND CUP OF WINE

INT. JERRY'S APARTMENT - NIGHT

ELAINE
What's next? Still no food, right?

JERRY
Nope.

KRAMER
Another glass of wine actually.

ELAINE
Of course. Why would we eat dinner at a dinner?

<u>EVERYONE:</u>

בָּרוּךְ אַתָּה ה', אֱ-לֹהֵינוּ מֶלֶךְ
הָעוֹלָם, בּוֹרֵא פְּרִי הַגָּפֶן.

Baruch atah Adonai, Eloheinu Melech ha'olam,
bo're p'ri hagafen.

Praised Are You, Our G-d, who creates the fruit of
the vine.

MOTZI-MATZO

GEORGE RE-ENTERS.

GEORGE

Quiet, quiet, Yael's coming. She's coming back right
now. She's giving me another chance.

JERRY

How'd you swing that?

GEORGE

She said in all her life she's never not eaten matzo
at a Seder before, so I told her she never has to see
me again, just come back, finish Seder, and eat
some matzo.

JERRY

And of course you didn't mean that.

GEORGE

I am the Wicked Child, Jerry.

YAEL RE-ENTERS, LOOKING AMBIVALENT,
ACTUALLY NOT TOO PLEASED ABOUT IT.

GEORGE

OK. OK. What's next, people? Let's keep this Seder
rolling.

KRAMER

It's time for the Motzi-Matzo. The blessing over and
then the eating of the matzo.

GEORGE

Perfect! Yael, want to lead us?

YAEL

Fine.

YAEL RELUCTANTLY RAISES ALL THE MATZO
ON THE SEDER PLATE.

YAEL

I raise all the matzo on the Seder plate.
And say that for seven days we shall only eat
unleavened bread. And now everyone says:

EVERYONE:

בָּרוּךְ אַתָּה ה', אֱ-לֹהֵינוּ מֶלֶךְ
הָעוֹלָם, הַמּוֹצִיא לֶחֶם מִן
הָאָרֶץ.

*Baruch atah Adonai, Eloheinu Melech ha'olam,
hamotzi lechem min ha'aretz.*

*Blessed Are You G-d, who brings forth bread from
the land.*

EVERYONE:

בָּרוּךְ אַתָּה יְיָ, אֱלֹהֵינוּ מֶלֶךְ הָעוֹלָם,
אֲשֶׁר קִדְּשָׁנוּ בְּמִצְוֹתָיו וְצִוָּנוּ עַל
אֲכִילַת מַצָּה

Baruch atah Adonai, Eloheinu Melech ha'olam,
asher kid-shanu b'mitzvotav v'tzivanu al achilat
matzah.

Blessed Are You, Our G-d, who blesses us with
mitzvot and instructs us to eat matzo.

MAROR/KORECH

GEORGE

And now, we eat the matzo in the Korech sandwich
with the Maror and the Charoset. Right? See, we're
noshing on matzo at Seder. I kept my promise, Yael.
Everyone's happy.

YAEL BRIGHTENS SLIGHTLY.

GEORGE

Yael, want to guide us through the prayer?

YAEL

Sure. The Maror symbolizes the bitter life of
slavery.

GEORGE

And the Charoset represents the mortar used by the
slaves to build the Pharaoh's cities.

YAEL FULLY BRIGHTENS, IMPRESSED WITH
GEORGE'S KNOWLEDGE. A CHANCE FOR HIM?

> YAEL
> That's right, Georgiah-Yitzhak.

YAEL CLUTCHES GEORGE'S HAND.

> ELAINE
> Mortar and tears, huh? Quite a party.

> GEORGE
> Shhh. Don't ruin this for me, Elaine.

97

EVERYONE:

בָּרוּךְ אַתָּה יי אֱלֹהֵינוּ מֶלֶךְ הָעוֹלָם,
אֲשֶׁר קִדְּשָׁנוּ בְּמִצְוֹתָיו וְצִוָּנוּ עַל
אֲכִילַת מָרוֹר

*Baruch atah Adonai, Eloheinu Melech ha'olam,
asher kid'shanu b'mitzvotav v'tzivanu al achilat
maror.*

*Blessed Are You Our G-d, who makes us holy with
mitzvot and commands us to eat the maror.*

EVERYONE TAKES A BITE OF THE KORECH.

YAEL

Wow, Kramer. This is the best matzo I've ever had.
It really does taste as good as bread. You must tell
me, what's your secret?

KRAMER

I'm glad you asked, Yael. The trick is baking soda.

SUDDENLY YAEL SPITS HER KORECH OUT.

YAEL

Baking soda! That means it's leavened, Kramer!
That means it's hametz! What have you done to me,
Kramer?!

GEORGE

What have you done to me, Kramer?!

KRAMER

But there's no yeast! I thought hametz just meant
no yeast! I swear there's no yeast, Yael!

YAEL

It's not just no yeast, you idiot!

GEORGE

I'm so sorry, Yael.

YAEL

This is all your fault, Georgiah-Yitzhak. Your Seder
has completely ruined my Passover! I am leaving
New York this instant for the homeland. In Israel,
men know how to treat women and they know how
to let themselves be treated by their parents. And
they certainly know what is and isn't matzo!

YAEL STORMS OUT.

GEORGE

Great! Just great.

ELAINE HAPPILY EATS THE "MATZO, NOT SO."

ELAINE

I don't know what her problem is. I think this stuff's
pretty good.

SHULCHAN OREICH

KRAMER

Well, at last it's time for the Shulchan Oreich!

ELAINE

For G-d's sake, is that the meal?

KRAMER

It is!

ELAINE

Praised is She!

ENJOY YOUR MEAL!!!

Whether it be mutton or fat-free frozen yogurt, Joe's mango or Joe's mackinaw peaches, brisket, pastrami, Junior Mints, Jujyfruits, Pez, or a big matzo ball hanging out...

Be sure to eat up, enjoy, and compliment the host(s).

THE POST-MEAL FESTIVITIES: THE TZAFUN, THE THIRD CUP, THE FOURTH CUP, AND THE WELCOMING OF ELIJAH

AFTER DINNER, JERRY CLEARS DISHES. THE GUESTS ARE GONE EXCEPT FOR GEORGE, ELAINE, AND KRAMER.

JERRY

What's the deal with The Afikomen? The Tzafun? First of all, pick one name for it. Second of all, you hide this thing somewhere in your house, under a dirty couch cushion, in a grimy corner of the kitchen, it gets filthy, then the kids eat it? Who thought that was a good idea?

GEORGE

Where's yours?

ELAINE LIFTS UP JERRY'S COUCH CUSHION.
INDEED, IT'S FILTHY, THERE ARE CRUMBS
EVERYWHERE. BUT JERRY'S UNFAZED.

JERRY

At least it's not burning.

ELAINE

That's the spirit.

GEORGE

It's time for the third glass.

ELAINE

It's actually my fifth with the Miriam and the extra
one with Ramses, but yeah, fill 'er up.

GEORGE FILLS THEIR GLASSES.

JERRY

Well, Kramer and Elaine may have each lost five million dollars and the chance at both of their businesses, and we may have ruined George's shot at a Sephardic woman, and ruined the poor Sephardic woman's Passover, not to mention my apartment, but I'd say the Seder was a huge success.

THEY CHEERS.

<u>EVERYONE:</u>

בָּרוּךְ אַתָּה ה', אֱ-לֹהֵינוּ מֶלֶךְ הָעוֹלָם, בּוֹרֵא פְּרִי הַגָּפֶן.

Baruch atah Adonai, Eloheinu Melech ha'olam, borei p'ri hagafen.

Praised Are You, Our G-d, who has created the fruit of the vine.

ELAINE GRABS HER COAT. KRAMER STOPS
HER FROM LEAVING.

ELAINE

Is there really more?

KRAMER

Yes!

JERRY

I think we say another blessing and drink another
glass of wine.

ELAINE

This is one crazy holiday you guys have for
yourselves.

GEORGE POURS ANOTHER ROUND. KRAMER
JUMPS UP SUDDENLY, SPILLS HIS WINE ALL
OVER JERRY'S CARPET.

KRAMER

There's also songs. I forgot the songs!

JERRY

No, Kramer! We're not singing songs! I'm drawing
the line at songs. No hugs, no lessons, no songs.

GEORGE

What about blessings and prayers?

JERRY

Fine. One more!

<u>EVERYONE:</u>

בָּרוּךְ אַתָּה ה', אֱ-לֹהֵינוּ מֶלֶךְ
הָעוֹלָם, בּוֹרֵא פְּרִי הַגָּפֶן.

*Baruch atah Adonai, Eloheinu Melech ha'olam,
borei p'ri hagafen.*

*Praised Are You, Our G-d, who has created the
fruit of the vine.*

ELAINE
Is <u>that</u> it?

JERRY
Should be. I'm just glad that a certain
you-know-who didn't show—

SUDDENLY, NEWMAN ENTERS.

JERRY
(grimacing)
Newman.

NEWMAN
You mean, Elijah Newman?

JERRY
(grimacing)
Elijah Newman.

KRAMER
This means the Messiah's coming!

NEWMAN

Not so fast. Where's my plate and goblet?

JERRY

It's right here.

NEWMAN

You're supposed to fill the plate and the goblet.
What am I supposed to do with an empty plate and
an empty goblet?

JERRY

Sorry, Newman, this is what you get. No full plate,
no full goblet.

NEWMAN

Fine. No Messiah.

JERRY

So be it. No Messiah.

JERRY SNATCHES AWAY THE EMPTY PLATE
AND THE EMPTY GOBLET.

NEWMAN MAKES A SQUEALING NOISE.

KRAMER

Would you two look at yourselves? You're arguing,
spiting each other, when we're talking about
bringing peace to the planet here! We're talking
about ending war. We're talking about Heaven on
Earth! Make him a plate, Jerry, fill his goblet!

JERRY

Oh alright!

JERRY PUTS DOWN THE PLATE AND THE
GOBLET AND OPENS HIS FRIDGE. NEWMAN
WHIPS OUT A BIB, SITS DOWN FOR HIS MEAL.

NEWMAN

Excellent.

THE CHAIR BREAKS. NEWMAN SQUEALS.

END OF SEDER/END OF SHOW

THE NIRZAH

DAVE COWEN[3]

And that's it. Time for the Nirzah. The conclusion of the Haggadah. What did you guys think?

JERRY

That was the best Haggadah ever written!

DAVE COWEN

Really?

LARRY

And the best Seinfeld episode ever written!

DAVE COWEN

Really?

JERRY

No!

---

[3] Author of this parody Haggadah.

LARRY

What are you, an idiot?!

DAVE COWEN

I'll try to do better next year, in Jerusalem!

END OF HAGGADAH

The Yada Yada Haggadah: A Sitcom Seder

Hebrew and English transliteration open-sourced from Wikipedia and Haggadot.com.

This book is written as a parody of the Seinfeld television show and as a teaching tool for Judaism. It is not authorized or endorsed by the creators, writers, producers, actors, or any of the companies or corporations involved in its production and distribution.

A portion of the profits will be donated to Jewish organizations in their honor.

The author, Dave Cowen, has published two other books:

The Trump Passover Haggadah

Fake History!: The Story Of How Christopher Columbus Was Treated Very Very Unfairly

Follow him at: amazon.com/author/davecowen

Made in the USA
Middletown, DE
11 April 2022